# Secret
# Powers
## *of This*
# World

TENA FRIERSON

**author**HOUSE®

AuthorHouse™
1663 Liberty Drive
Bloomington, IN 47403
www.authorhouse.com
Phone: 833-262-8899

Published by AuthorHouse  01/27/2025

ISBN: 979-8-8230-4190-4 (sc)
ISBN: 979-8-8230-4191-1 (hc)
ISBN: 979-8-8230-4189-8 (e)

Library of Congress Control Number: 2025901545

Print information available on the last page.

Scripture quotations marked KJV are from the Holy Bible, King James Version
(Authorized Version). First published in 1611. Quoted from the KJV Classic
Reference Bible, Copyright © 1983 by The Zondervan Corporation.

# Contents

# Introduction

I was brought up in a small town in South Carolina were there were some strange activities that happened in my life growing up as a child. This book is about my experiences I have been through as well as some of my family members. My grandparents practice witchcraft which has opening doors that should have kept closed. Most Christians are ignorant of Satan's kingdom, they don't believe it really exist, even the ones who go to church on a regular basis. If you don't deal with Satan and his servants, they will deal with you. There is knowledge about Satan's Kingdom that God want to release to Christians most don't want the information. God said in Hosea 4:6 "My people perish because of lack of knowledge." That's why Satan and his servants are getting away with so much in this world because Christians that do know that witchcraft are real, they are afraid to take up their authority in Jesus to fight back. If you are a pastor and you don't do spiritual combat against the demonic, please do yourself a favor and step down until your get some power and courage to do what you are called to do, if you say you were called by God. Another important topic in this book I talk a little on politics. Some people don't believe that Christians should be in politics, take it from me you should want Christians in politics representing the things of God. If not, we will eventually be destroyed like Sodom and Gomorrah. Face it this country is heading down like a fallen sparrow because people have been taking God our creator out of everything believing that their hands have gotten them their wealth. But when disaster hit their lives, they will be calling on his name to help them in their time of need. Politics is very important because it doesn't just effect one person, it effects a whole nation. We need our leaders to support God values and morals because anything else will be a disaster. Some leaders in US have gotten so polluted to the point that they have passed laws for homosexuals to marry one another. Showing the world that it's normal to practice sodomy in America what I am trying to say is there is no life in this but death. As we can see the world is calling the good bad and what's bad good.

# 1

## *Familiar Spirits*

Growing up as a child I can't believe the things I still remember so clear as being so young I had some scary experiences things I saw with my own eyes and couldn't understand at the time concerning the supernatural during that time the first house I was born in I thought the house was haunted because I use to see evil spirits almost all that time I found out later the true meaning once I became a Christian these things had happen because my grandparents had opening doors that had release demons in our lives and home during my childhood I could remember my decease great grandmother would visit us late at night she would knock on the door before she enter the room she would walk past my bed into the other room were the other sleep and she would sit in the old red rocking chair and rock until morning light this had continue for a while before she stop on some days me and my siblings would be playing outside and would see her watching us from the window inside of the house.

# 2

## *Chaos*

People in general don't understand when a family member dabble in the occult it don't just affect them it effect the whole generation I can recalled many times on the weekend my grandparents would argue and fight constantly when my grandfather comes home drunk they would fight like cats and dogs and would break furniture and artifacts that my uncle made in school we would wake up the next day the house would be in shambles with blood on the artifacts and walls it was awful to see grandparents fight like they were young it is bad when young people do it but it is crazy when old folks behave like that I had never heard them said anything good to each other it was always negative it didn't took long to see they had a love hate relationship.

# 3

## *Out in the Night*

As a child, I can remember going to bed at night, but what has frightened me was something would bring me back home and put me through the window.

I had never seen what it looked like that took me out into the night.

I could only remember coming back through the window.

I would be so cold and scared as I walked back into my room and climbed in my bed, and no one had ever noticed I was gone.

Until this day, that still puzzles me that something would take me from my home, and I did not remember where I've been.

God saved me from whatever that was because eventually it stopped.

God was working in my favor even as a child so evil could not do to me what it wanted to.

# 4

## *Roots*

My mother did not like her mother burning roots.

That was the name of the practice she done.

It's when you burn roots to get something done in your favor from demons, spirits.

My granny told everyone in the house to never plunder in her room because we might see something that we didn't want to see.

Me and my siblings used to plunder in her room for snacks.

And one day we discovered seeing roots in her room by doing what she told us not to do after I saw that ugly looking thing again, I stop looking for snack after that

But let me recall, my first experience of seeing this as a child, I was sitting on a step on the porch on the backside of the house and the sun was shining down on a jar outside on a shelf in front of the barn.

4

I walked up to the jar and had picked up a tobacco stick and knocked the jar to the ground.

And I saw a brownish, syrup looking color inside the jar.

I saw eyes that was alive and moving in the jar.

I never saw anything so evil before.

Then from out of nowhere, a man came from behind the barn.

No human could have fit behind those trees and bushes.

He told me to leave the jar alone.

I had just known that the roots were my granddaddy own, and my grandmama kept hers in the house, in her room.

By me seeing what I have saw and knowing it, was my grandfather.

I never looked at my grandparents the same

I say to myself, what in the world have they gotten themselves into?

I was kind of afraid of them.

# 5

## *The River Road*

The area where we used to live when I was a child was called the River Road

It was an area where some people lost their life, mostly from car accidents during the 70s.

I could remember sometimes coming home with my family at night.

I would see dead spirits, sometimes walking down the road.

I can recall on some occasion seeing a man with his head off his body.

I didn't panic during that time because I thought that everyone in the car could see him too.

There were many nights when we returned home and I saw dead bodies on the porch, lying by the door.

I had to walk past them to get in the house.

During that time in my life, it seemed normal seeing dead spirits until I was older and knew the difference.

# 6

## *Moving*

The time has come when my family had moved

That was the end of the 70s.

I was so glad to leave that haunted house.

But later, I find out that it was not the house.

It was the people that I was connected to.

The house we moved into was on a long dirt road by the woods, surrounded by fields.

We had so many roaches and no matter what was done to remove them, it did not work

We had a high volume of mosquitoes.

Even if we built a smoke fire, it did not do any good because it was too many, which hinder us from playing outside during those times.

# 7

## *Evil Spirits*

Here I go again.

Different house, but the same scenario.

At 3am, I would awaken like clockwork to see a night hag over my older sister.

I would ask God, "Why do you wake me up to see this?"

When I could not do anything at that time, but look, because I did not know spiritual warfare then.

I would mention it to my sister about those evil spirits over her at night, but she never believed me.

My mother worked on evening shifts during that time and my aunt would discipline us when needed.

She will tell me to bed if I misbehave and many times I did and went straight to bed.

I would leave the lights on to keep out the demonic spirits until my mother got home, but that did not work.

8

It did not stop Zorro, the demon.

When I would get sent to bed early, I would get attacked by this demonic spirit called Zorro.

I could be lying in the bed as he would come closer, my body would begin to stiffen to the point where I could not move.

I would scream and no one was able to hear me.

Even if I was in a house full of people, I had this attack several times and I got tired of him putting me into a trance.

On this certain night I had to see him.

How the spirit looked

When it entered, I fought with all I had to keep my eyes open.

I saw him and he was wearing a black and red cape with a black hat and an eye mask.

Just like Zorro, his eyes were red, and he would take his cape and spread it all around me.

As he pressed his weight on my body, I called on the name of Jesus, he would leave instantly, but he continued to torment me for a while before he stopped, and other spirits came to visit throughout my life.

parents, when your child say that they have seen the boogeyman, believe me, they can see them.

Take it from me.

There are things that go bump in the night.

*Tena Frierson*

The Lord has allowed me to remember all these things that happened to me as a child to write this book, to educate Christians and others about the reality of demonic spirits all around us that makes visitation sometimes in the natural realm.

And some of you readers would think that this book is a fairy tale that I made up, but these are events that has taken place in my life.

# 8

## *Awareness*

When demons would first start to harass me, I would call on the name of God and they hesitated until I said, "In the name of Jesus."

Then I learned that there is power in the name of Jesus Christ.

Remember this, at the time I was not saved and did not know too much about the Bible.

But once I got saved, all of this made sense to me.

It fell into a puzzle that fit.

When you read the Bible, it talks about demon spirits and what role they play in people's lives, whether they are aware of them or not.

When Jesus and the disciples cast out demons out of people, they did not go to hell.

They are here today roaming around us.

They are trying to entice us to do evil, to keep us sinning, so that we will miss heaven.

Another thing that demons do is to keep us focused on everything all around us except God.

How could we protect ourselves from them by not being ignorance of the devil devices and how he operates, realizing that they are here to kill, steal, and destroy our lives.

Most Christians do not believe that they can have a demon.

Most Christians do not believe that the disciples were casting out demons from Christians during the Bible days.

Most Christians believe that if a demon was in them, they would be forming out of the mouth and talking in deep scary voices.

No, that is when they are possessed.

Christians cannot be possessed because that's when the demon takes control over their minds and body.

But Christians can have a demon that takes control over a certain area in their body that they gave them the power to have.

They can have anything that they open themselves up to.

When you are disobedient to God, in Ecclesiastes 10 states, if you break a hedge, the serpent will bite you.

I believe that people during the Bible time had known a lot about demonic spirits than this generation because this woman states in Mark 7:26 that her child is vexed with a demon.

And when Jesus rebuked the fever, he called it a demon spirit and commanded it to come out of the people.

How Many Christians will call their sickness a demon, not many.

They will dress it up and make it sound pretty than what it is.

Most of the time they will remain sick or die when all they must do is put the axe at the root of the tree.

I am going back to Jesus rebuking the fever

what does that sound like to you?

Deliverance.

That is what missing in most all churches except a few that does minister deliverance.

When Christians get saved, they don't stay saved if they don't confess their sins.

If they don't confess their sins, there is no deliverance.

When you get saved, you must open your mouth and don't just assume that God will read your mind.

No, confessing, no deliverance.

Because all the demons will do is go down deep inside of you and fester, then rise back up then your old urges return then you turn back into the world.

One of the real reasons why Christians don't get delivered is because they do not think that they need it and that it is someone else and not them.

Romans 12:3 says, don't think so highly of yourself than you ought to.

Be humble minded and you will get further in God.

He can do a lot in our life when we are not operating in a prideful spirit

Pride hinder deliverance

Satan greatest accomplishments is keeping pastors and Christians in the dark about demonic spirits and evil spirits fallen angels

If they are not brought into the light, they will continue in darkness, hiding in our lives and we are calling them something else instead of calling them what they are.

I wish that most Christians will come to the next level in God with supernatural knowledge so we can be affected towards Satan kingdom.

One of the main reasons why the church service is so full of work with no power and singing songs about the Holy Spirit is welcome, which is just words because the body of Christ is ignorance of Satan devices that he used to keep the real power of God out of the churches.

And we end up with natural works operating in church services.

The letter kills, but it the spirit that gives life.

When some Christians come across other Christians who is walking in power and the supernatural in God, they look strange to them.

Do you know why people like that is so effective in the kingdom of God?

Because they have true revelation about evil spirits.

They know how to fight them they gain more ground than the average Christians.

Most Pastors do not think demonic evil spirits fallen spirits is in their churches.

because they are probably in them and their members.

One of the ways that you can recognize a demon inside of you is by problems that you can't seem to break for example ungodly urges that keep churning inside of you that you can't seem to get rid of.

Like homosexuality?

They think that God intend for them to be that way because they are attracted to the same sex.

Do you know why they are attracted to one another?

There are homosexual demonic spirits that give off sex urges to be with the same sex.

These demons keep showing up in the bloodline because the forefathers had never repented to God for that sin.

God allows Satan to keep sending demonic spirits in their generation until someone gets saved and repent to God for that sin.

In the book of Deuteronomy 5:9 what would happen is that the demons would skip one of the siblings and enter the other one.

This will continue throughout each generation in the bloodline until repentance occurs.

To bring the kingdom of God to the earth, you will have to come against demonic forces.

I believe the reason people cannot get revelation about evil spirits is because of their perception of them.

# 9

## *Visitors in Dreams*

When your eyes are close, and you are dreaming you are in the spiritual realm.

Did you ever hear the saying that things come in the spirit first before it comes in the natural?

One night while I was sleeping a man tried to break into my house.

I saw him first in a vision.

I said how did you get in here because I did not let you in.

I told him to leave my house in Jesus's name and he left.

When I woke up the next day, I noticed that my door has been tampered with and I thought about my vision.

Did you know that by supernatural intervention I had prevented my house from being broken into.

What Satan had planned for bad God turned it into good.

Whenever we pray to God in faith, he sent angels to fight off the demonic spirits that is in operation in people who are being influenced by demonic spirits to cause harm, the battle is fought in the spirit realm to protect us in the natural realm.

For example, in the book of Judges in chapter 4:21 it states about Deborah defeating Cicero the enemy.

Then in Judges 5:20 it states that the stars which is angels from heaven fought from their courses against Cicero.

as you can see there were a spiritual battle going on which had result in the victory of defeating Cicero in the natural.

# 10

## *Satan Kingdom*

When it comes to Satan Kingdom, most people do not really believe that the devil is real.

Why do you think that so many demonic movies are on television?

If you see them that way you will never take up your authority over them.

Satan knows that very well.

# 11

## *We are Spiritual Beings*

We are made up of body, soul, and spirit.

When you die, you become a full spirit.

And if you just caught the relation about spirits after you die, it is too late.

I must tell you how to save your life and your loved ones.

Sometimes evil spirits can kill you in your sleep and you will not wake up.

They can scare you unto death in your sleep.

If they could come to you in the night season through your dreams, vision just rebuked them and commanded them to leave in Jesus's name.

I also believe God gave a lot of people knowledge about what Satan was trying to do to a loved one, or friend.

They would dream that they die, and they would wake up and say, "Oh, so and so is going to die."

Not thinking that they could be dying before they time.

God said, "What is hidden?

He will bring to the rooftop."

God sometimes show us what Satan is trying to do behind the scenes.

If you get a dream like that and you believe it is not their time to die, cancel the dream in Jesus name from coming to pass.

But for some of you who think you cannot die before your time, what about suicide?

God gave all of us a will and choices.

Our choice leads us down the road.

We choose and if you choose to believe that Satan plots are not real, you are already defeated.

# 12

## *Baptism*

I started going to church when I was 13.

My oldest sister and brother were going before me.

When I got baptized, my siblings did as well.

I know at the time, people were telling us, that we need to be baptized?"

The day I got baptized at our family church, the water was very cold that morning and I was 14 at the time.

Once we got inside for the ceremony, I was standing at the front of the church when suddenly, I start to see colors flashing before my eyes.

I started looking around the church as to what was going on.

I heard a quiet voice in my spirit telling me, "Do not be afraid.

I had this peace that came over me."

Then I noticed everything started getting dark until I was completely blind.

God started talking to me.

As he talked to me, I had this peace that I cannot explain.

When he finished talking, light came back to my sight and all the colors started flashing back into my eyes.

Then I could see again.

Not only could I see, but I had also believed my vision had gotten better than what it was.

After high school, I went through a time of pain and hurting, trying to find my identity of who I was and what would become of me.

I can recall drinking alcohol, but mostly on the weekends trying to drown my sorrows, but as you know, that do not work.

The pain remains once you get sober.

# 13

## *Hell*

I was heading down the wrong road making decisions that would hurt me rather than help me.

One night after I was drinking with a friend of mines, when I got home, I fell asleep, and I woke up in hell.

As I was standing there, I knew where I was.

You would have all your senses.

I could hear, smell, taste, and feel.

What I had felt was hopelessness.

I cannot describe to you in words.

It's far beyond what most humans could ever think of.

You cannot imagine being in a place where there is no love at all.

I had said to myself, "I won't see my family anymore.

I watch souls being torment by the devil."

Hell was a huge cage in the ground.

The air was so hot that you cannot hardly breathe.

I saw people who practiced witchcraft change from animals to back to themselves.

I saw men and women of all races bound in chains being torment by the devil.

I had said to myself why I am not being torment.

Then I heard God's voice that sounded like thunder.

He said, you are just visiting,

But if you do not give your life to me, this is where you will end up."

I was put back into my body.

I woke up with my heart beating so fast, I feared what I had just experienced.

I told myself the next day I was not going to mention this to no one.

While I was in the kitchen, one of my siblings entered.

I heard a voice that told me to tell what I had experienced that night before.

I told the dream, and that person said that he had went to hell also.

Satan was tormenting him God had confirmed to us both that the dream was real.

When I had first entered hell in the dream, I had said to myself if I did not murder or kill anyone, so why am I here?

That's how a lot of people think today.

They feel that by their own standards of how they see themselves, that they do not deserve to go to hell.

Because the biggest sin people believe is murder, which God can forgive anybody if they will repent.

The reason why we go to hell is because we do not accept Jesus as our personal Savior.

And if we don't try to live the way He wants us to, people feel like they can say anything and do whatever they want and still get into heaven.

But that's not true.

God does not make us do anything that we do not want to do.

That's why He gave us a will.

If we don't make it into heaven, it is not His fault that we have allowed anything to distract us and we miss God.

After my hell experience, I had walked around in wilderness for weeks.

The Lord says, if you hear me, knock, open the door

By being so young at that time, I did harden my heart.

God was only trying to save me from something later down the road.

When the time has come, I had hit a wall and I say, this is what the Lord was trying to save me from.

As I was staring death in the face, I had nowhere to look but up.

God had got my complete attention, and I gave my life to Him.

I was very glad I did.

Oh, but His mercy and grace?

I am so thankful Jesus died on the cross for us all so we could have a chance to make it to heaven.

The choice is ours.

Some people will not accept God even after they saw God do miracles in their life.

They love the world more than they love Him.

God say, if you love anything more than me, you are not worthy of me.

When I got saved, I was going to my first husband church.

I was a new believer, and I was so thirsty for knowledge about God.

I had read my Bible from beginning to end and did not understand most of it.

I pray and ask the Lord for understanding.

Then someone told me that I need to receive the Holy Spirit because He is the teacher of the word.

I had fasted and prayed and believed God and He had filled me when He got ready.

I know a lot of Christians believe that if the minister lay hands on you that you would receive the Holy Spirit instantly.

But that's not true.

God will fill you when He is ready.

No matter what anybody tells you, God do not want us to take the Holy Spirit lightly.

He knows the condition of man's heart.

# 14

## *Behind the Scenes*

The main thing about Satan's kingdom is getting you to do things that they want us to do and you not realizing that it's them.

Unlike some people who know they are working for Satan kingdom, here are some examples of how Satan influenced people on your job.

you never did anything to this person, and they hate you without a cause.

They tried to turn people against you with bad mouth when they get a chance.

The sad thing is they don't know it's a demonic spirit in the realm that is talking to them to do what they want.

Demons love to cause dissensions among us to keep us upset and bitter, hating by stirring up any kind of evil between us to keep us separated.

The issues whites and blacks.

The evil one knows if we all get along, Satan will have problems in his kingdom.

Do you remember when 911 happened?

Did you notice how most of us gotten alone?

There was love for one another.

It was like our color of our skin did not matter.

I believe that the devil said that this must stop because if this continues, God will come down from heaven and reveal himself to mankind.

Satan said, "I must keep them separated."

he started by injecting thoughts back into mankind's mind and they fell back on to the devil's plan.

In this society white people are more favored than any other race.

How do I know I am right?

Because society put it in front our faces.

Actions speak louder than words.

Satan Kingdom has no respectable person.

He plays both sides.

Demonic spirits tell black people, "Do you see how whites are treating you wrong?"

Then he plays the white people by injecting negative thoughts in their head about the blacks.

This goes on and on.

If God wanted us to look the same, he would have made us the same.

If we look at his creation, everything does not look the same.

It looks like its own kind.

Everything God made is good.

If you think different kinds of races are bad because you do not like the way they look, take it up with your creator, God himself.

God does not want us to hate one another, but to love one another.

How can we say that we love God who we never seen and can't love the people we see every day?

Love would conquer all multitudes of hate.

God hates the spirit of pride.

Romans 12:3.

God says, "Don't think so highly of yourself that you are unable to associate with people of low character."

White ministers, if you have prejudice in you, pray to God to deliver you from that evil spirit.

Don't just continue to stand in God's house as he approves of you.

That goes for black preachers also and other races.

If each individual starts standing up for one another, when we hear a prejudice statement, we will shame the devil and put a stop to that evil spirit.

# 15

## *The Conference*

A week before the Lord had filled me with his Holy Spirit, Satan came to me in a vision.

I saw him outside of my house by the window.

He was looking at me with an anger look.

The look in his eyes was pitch black.

He came in the form of a young white man.

I could feel his anger because he knew how powerful the Holy Spirit is over him.

The night when I received the Holy Spirit, I was in my bed sleeping and I felt a rushing wind come in my room and I heard the Lord's voice say, "Don't be afraid.

This is me."

I felt electricity come inside of me and that's when all the dreams and visions start occurring.

Before I went to the conference out of town, I was having dreams of witches.

I did not understand the dream until later.

A couple ladies I went to church with, and others was on the van

When this lady got on the van, I heard in my spirit that she was one of the ladies I saw in my dream that was a witch.

She was on an assignment from the devil.

Her and a lot of witches came to the conference to see what God was doing in the meeting.

Their job was to destroy us spiritually.

You will meet different people at conferences pretending to be Christians, but they are witches.

They disguise themselves as Christians.

Most of them will try to gain your trust.

They will ask to pray for you by laying their hands on you.

Once you allow them to touch you, they will transfer a demonic spirit to you, and you will notice a change in your body.

Once the demon inside of you, you will want it out because there will be a change in your behavior, and you will know it.

They love to pray on young believers so you will not have a successful life in the Lord.

This is how you will know if they place a demon inside of you.

33

You will not be able to read your Bible, and you have a hard time praying.

And sometimes you will start experiencing pain inside of your body that started when they touched you.

A demon would be the last thing you would think of that was causing you problems.

How many people would tell the demon to leave them?

Almost no Christians would because they think highly of themselves than they ought to.

But the scriptures say if you break a hedge, the serpent will bite you.

The hedge was broken when you allowed them to lay hands on you.

Why do you think God put these scriptures in the Bible to protect us from demonic people being used by Satan and his servants?

Once they lay hands on you, you have sinned, and you did not discern the spirit operating in them and you gave them permission to transfer the evil spirits inside of you.

God people must know how easy it is to be deceived

Whenever you go out of town to a church conference, be very careful.

2Corinthians 11:13 states, "For such are false apostles, deceitful workers masquerading as apostle of Christ

And no wonder if his servants, masquerading as servants of righteousness, their end will be what their actions deserve."

There are some people who know that they are serving Satan, and their job is to pretend that they are Christians to deceive us.

They dress like us, try to act like Christians, pretending so we could trust them.

The devil must trick us to get us.

They will not show us their identity because we will want nothing to do with them and they know that.

# 16

## *Spiritual Warfare*

There was a minister that came to church that

I was attending.

She has said something so dumb.

She said there is no need for spiritual warfare.

If there is no need for spiritual warfare, why do we pray?

When you are praying against demonic spirits, commanding them to leave you or the person.

You are praying spiritual warfare in case you didn't know.

Let me define spiritual warfare.

It's a battle going on in the spirit world.

Demons that attack our bodies but when we pray to God, He will send the angels to fight off the demonic spirits

That's affecting us.

For instance, all sickness is coming from demonic spirits.

All we do is feed them pills.

In the New Testament, what do you think Jesus and His disciples were demonstrating?

When they were praying for people, they were commanding the evil spirits to leave the people who were sick and possessed.

Once the demons left, they were healed and delivered.

Jesus said greater works we will be able to do because He went to the Father.

John 14:12.

We will cast out demons and lay hands on the sick and they will be healed.

Matthew 10:8.

Jesus is talking about demonic spirits that affect our lives daily.

Most Christians are lazy, and they don't want to deal with demonic spirits.

They will say Jesus bear it all on the cross.

Jesus laid down the foundation for us to do what He is doing.

When you get saved, it is not the time to be lazy.

It's time to go to work.

Not just sitting in a church every Sunday and Wednesday gaining all that information and knowledge and doing nothing with it.

# 17

## *Relationships*

My first marriage ended up in divorce because my husband had a lot of anger issues that he did not deal with.

You cannot make a person change.

You can pray all you want, but it still comes down to a person's will.

God said that he wished that all will be saved, but it still comes down to choice

My next relationship, I had ended up pregnant with my daughter.

I know now that he was just a distraction that was trying to pull me away from the things of God.

It seemed to work for a while, but I had snapped out of it and broke off the relationship and later found out some disturbing news about him that he had kept from me, so it all worked out on the end for the best.

I had repented to God, asked him to forgive me and cleanse me from everything that I had opened doors to in my life.

I am not making up excuses for my actions.

I know that the only way God can deliver us is if we are open and honest about everything, confessing the things that we are doing wrong, so we won't revisit our past mishaps.

I know when some Christians put themselves on pedestals, they feel that they have an image to uphold like they are flawless.

I know when they fall into sin, they must cover it up quickly so no one will know when women and men have babies out of wedlock.

Some have abortions if they are leaders in the church.

Some parents will make their daughter kill the unborn child because of the image they seem to portray in their church.

It is sad when some will value what people think than God.

When people gossip about someone having a baby out of wedlock, it will soon end up on their own doorstep.

Whether it will be them, or their grandchild will end up pregnant.

People who had gossiped about me had ended up pregnant also.

The Lord told me the measure that they judge you He will judge them by that same measure.

Matthew 7:2.

Be careful before you speak.

Make sure nothing is found in you.

# 18

## *Ungodly*

Did you know when you kill your unborn child by abortions you are making a human sacrifice to Satan?

Did you know that it is written in the Old Testament?

Satan influenced people to sacrifice their child to the God of Chemosh

(Jeremiah 7:31) God say they had built the high places at Tophet which is in the valley of Son of Hanon to burn the son and daughter in the fire which I command them not.

Neither did it came into my heart.

In this generation Satan must trick you to deceive you.

He got people to kill their unborn child by presenting the baby as a bunch of tissue.

In God eyes when the sperm connects to the egg the baby becomes life.

Satan got the government to pass a bill to kill unborn babies which is the gun, and the parents are the one who pulls the trigger which has created genocides in our nation.

I believe if this nation doesn't repent, we will suffer for all the unborn babies going back up to God when He had a plan for each child here on earth no matter how they were conceived.

God say be aware of the devil devices He used to deceive us but if we do not spend time with our Lord nor read the Bible how will we know what He likes and dislikes?

You will be judging from the world's standards and not from God's standards and that is the only one that counts.

Let's define worldly standards.

Standards that you feel are right.

Proverbs 14:12 the way that seems right to man which always leads to death.

Do you want godly people in government office or ungodly people that would please men instead of having God standards?

Now if you choose ungodly people because they can bring you wealth that will do you no good when God is finished with us.

Ezekiel 7:19 states your love of money has gotten your nation destroyed.

They had thrown their money in the streets because of the suffering they were inflicted with.

The money did them no good once the wrath of God came upon them.

The people in Jeremiah time did not believe that their city could be destroyed no matter what they did.

God sent Jeremiah the prophet to prophesize to the people in Jerusalem to repent from worshiping other gods and idols and to turn back to him, but they refused.

He spoke with several leaders many times, but they believed they could serve God and worship false idols.

When God pronounced Jerusalem to be destroyed the spiritual leaders during that time was against what Jeremiah was saying.

They say that Jeremiah was lying, and God was not going to destroy them because he was pleased with them.

The false prophets that was close to the king stated that God pronounced blessings for them sound just like Americans today.

God is telling Americans to change their ways and repent to him.

Did you know that God had established the government, but it does not function the way he planned?

Today we want politicians who can make us richer.

Some people believe that Christians should not be in office.

you rather have ungodly leaders in Washington making laws against your God.

How long do you believe we will continue to be blessed in the United States?

Not long.

For instance, if ungodly leaders get in the office who promotes gay marriage and before you know it, gay marriages will become legal in all 50 states.

Which did happen while in the process of writing this book.

Which I was not surprised because of the direction I see this country heading.

Television will play an important role of changing some people's minds on how they view homosexuals.

The more they see it on television, the more some will become comfortable with it and their minds will be conform.

# 19

## *Concerning Politics*

If God had destroyed Sodom and Gomorra for that same lifestyle, do you think that America gets to exempt?

We are already in the process of judgment in this nation.

The bad storms we are having today is not a coincidence and other things that have happened

is because of Americans don't take God serious enough, and many people end up losing their life because of some Americans' ignorance towards God.

Nothing is new under the sun.

If you ever notice, a nation will become blessed and later starts to turn from God, will end up ruined.

During election time, I could remember having a conversation with a Christian brother about people who are in office who do not stand for the things of God.

He told me that we are supposed to submit to our government authorities no matter what they do because of Romans 13.

Let me clear up some misconceptions in the body of Christ.

We should obey the government only when they are not coming against the things of God.

If God says homosexuals are wrong and it's an abomination and killing your unborn baby is murder, that's what it is no matter what the government laws say.

If you are a real Christian, you have to say what God is saying no matter what the consequences is, but you do it with love

When the day comes and destruction is all around us, America, please don't call it nothing else.

But your decision that you have made by belittling the things of God, taking them lightly, has gotten this country to that place.

Time out for excuses, America.

What about Adolf Hitler when he was in the government?

And there was a Christian man named Dietrich Bonhoeffer who had found out the truth about Hitler and went to the Christian churches to warn them.

But they quoted Romans 13, obey your government authorities so they obey them and look where it got them.

# 20

## *Politics*

American people, we need to ask ourselves this question.

Why are the Republicans and Democrats keep fighting one another?

And nothing seems to be getting done.

I believe that most politicians are on the devil side.

It looks like they are bringing this country down on purpose to bring in the New World Order, which is a plan from Satan himself.

How do you think that Satan will accomplish this goal through the government system?

Let's keep paying attention to what they are showing us.

Our politicians in Washington mostly are getting rich for making deals against American people, rather than being for us.

Remember this, money do not just leave the earth, it just switches hands.

When President Bill Clinton was in office before, he left, he had made a trade law agreement with China.

And it came in effect while President Bush was president.

What that means that most of their supplies came here to the United States less our products went out to them.

Washington helped close most of our businesses here at that time for cheap cost from China.

Ask yourself this question, why we can't make our own products in this country which will put almost everybody back to work?

But if you ask the leaders in Washington, they will make up excuses why they cannot.

Sounds personal to me.

What it boils down to is help shut down this world money system and once it comes to an end, bring it back up again but only on their terms where there will be no more Republicans and Democrats.

The world will be on one government system, the new world order.

And your rights as a Christian will be gone because this is Satan system.

# 21

## *Elections*

Have you ever wanted something so bad that once you find out that God is not in it, you justify it enough times in your head to make it right with you?

I believe that God was not pleased with Christians who voted for President Obama.

We as Christians should have been praying for more godly candidates to run for presidents.

Obama does not stand for the principles of God, even when Christians find out that he supported abortions, they turn their heads the other way.

During his first and second term, he had a party for homosexual at the White House.

On the news, they say that this had never happened before by any other president.

Before he was elected, he told people that he was a Christian, but his action is really telling who he really worked for.

Everybody who applied for a job in America is required to show their ID, which includes social security card, driving license, and birth certificate.

Why President Obama at that time would not show his credentials unless he had something to hide.

That should have told us that something was not right.

I think that the 2008 presidency elections were too easy.

We had no good candidates running against President Obama.

The whole United States were a million of people and that was all we had.

I believe that it was more things going on behind the scenes that we know that have won him that election.

If someone were really going to make a difference to help the underprivileged, the devil would have fight them hands down if they had really had good intentions to help the people in this country.

I believe that the black Americans thought that that's why they voted for President Obama.

They voted for him and Satan knows how bad blacks wanted a black president.

Don't get me wrong.

I am for a black president but not that one.

The devil knows that once Obama got elected, no matter what wrong he does, they would pay him no attention.

Satan knows that this is one of the greatest ideals he could ever come up with by putting his ideals in a black leader that people look up to.

President Obama tried to bring in the mark of the beast system to the United States and help made it law through the health care bill.

I find out during that time that between the pages of 1010 in the document, it stated that all Americans must get a chip in them by their health care provider stating that it was for medical records, which is a lie.

God say in Revelation 13 in the Bible that without the mark of the beast, you cannot buy and sell and in other words, you cannot see a doctor without that chip

It didn't come out in the open yet, but it will come out for sure.

The government already got things in place and signs is all around us.

It is sad that most people are distracted

Most politicians look nice in their fancy clothes and their fake smiles arguing on TV with each other trying to look serious like they are doing us a favor.

most of it is just a show while in the dark rooms making deals of how, they are going to destroying this country.

# 22

## *Picking Up Evil Spirits*

Did you know you can pick up evil spirits from certain places?

They can attach themselves to you that how they enter your home.

I remember a time when I was visiting my cousin one night when it was time for me to leave.

Soon as I got in my car, I felt a present came in.

I could see a dark shadow of a man, but I was not sure.

All the way home, I felt someone in the car with me.

My husband at the time had worked night shift.

On that night, as soon as he came home, he started arguing for nothing.

The evil spirit in my home at the time had wanted us to argue.

he used both of us to carry out his plans to bring division between us.

During the argument, I left out of the bedroom to another room to go to sleep.

Soon as I started to fall asleep, I had opened my eyes, and I saw a black man shadow spirit that was standing at my bed.

I was surprised at what I was seeing.

Then it dawned on me that the present I felt at my cousin's house and in the car came in my house when I entered.

I shouted, "Go in the name of Jesus!"

Then it disappeared and left.

Most of the time, people cannot see evil spirits that are trying to cause trouble in their lives.

They are on assignment in the invisible realm that you cannot see.

Satan comes only to kill stealing the destroy people's lives, trying to keep us from being happy and living out God's purposes and destiny.

Our battle is not against flesh and blood, but it is against spiritual wickedness in high places that try to make our life difficult as possible.

Bad thoughts that are coming in our mind are coming from evil spirits.

You must resist them, and they will flee.

The things that I am writing about are the things that I have experienced. demonic spirits are real, and they are on this earth trying to destroy us

Christians must ask God for the gift of discernment so they will not be ignorant of the devil devices that he used to deceive us.

I had a bad experience with a Christian who claimed he belonged to the Lord.

One day we were talking at work about church matters and at the end of the conversation he reached out and shake my hand.

Once he did that, I felt something strange things start to happen.

I start seeing birds, shadows flying in the air in the spirit

I would rebuke them in the name of Jesus, and they will return.

While driving in the car, I could see cars coming into my land.

Like I wasn't there, almost hitting me.

I could feel an evil presence all around me on every side.

I was tired of the harassment, so I commanded the curse to be broken, and I send it back to the sender

I heard preachers say do not send curses back from people who send them, but I had tried everything I could think of to get rid of the torment.

It had stopped once I say that, and things went back to normal.

When I saw that person again, I told him about what had happened to me when we shook hands.

I questioned him about it, but he denied it like Satan people going to tell the truth.

If they do, they cannot deceive you anymore.

What had happened was once we shook hands; he transferred a curse to me.

That handshake was an evil agreement.

So, I had just agreed with what he wanted to do to me.

Out of ignorance, you cannot shake witches and warlords' hand, and you cannot hug them or else they would curse you.

# 23

## *Pretending Saints*

There is this old lady that I know.

She is very accepted in her community and church as a good Christian.

When she talks, she uses Jesus and God's name.

She would tell me stories about when people come against her.

God will punish them, but it was not God, it was Satan because she is a witch.

The preacher in her church, nor the members, has no idea who she really is because they are sent to the churches in their community to do the works of the devil.

They have gained everybody trust to deceive them.

When the people think that they are praying for them, they are placing curses on them because of association.

They dress like Christians; they seem modest and upstanding.

Some of you might think, "How can Satan people call on God and say Jesus if they are not Christians?

They are trained on how to deceive the body of Christ by attending the school of Satan."

Witchcraft people can say God and the name of Jesus, but they are talking about their god, Satan.

They call him Jesus while they are praying and worshiping to throw the average Christian off if they are in a church setting.

I know it sounds hard to understand, but like the scriptures say, Satan comes like an angel of light.

You must know who you are fellowshipping with.

That's one of the reasons the church has no power, just a good sounding sermon.

There is little healing in the church and much chaos and bickering at one another.

Preachers think that their churches are the best and they condemn other ministries.

Christians fight against each other gossiping, lying, having cliques and groups, thinking that they are better than other members while putting them down.

If they do not have money, they don't want to socialize with them.

Does that sound like chaos to you?

Don't you think that we should know better than that?

So why don't we act like we do?

Pastors pray to the Lord to show you the witches that are sent to your church and pray against their powers.

If you don't deal with them, they will deal with you and your members.

For some of you Christians who say, "I do not want to deal with witches' demonic spirits or any kind of evil."

You will never grow and be affected in the kingdom of God.

# 24

## *Handwriting on the Wall*

In the book of Daniel, he talks about handwriting on the wall.

King Belshazzar drunk out the Lord vessels that was taken from the Lord's temple.

When his father, King Nebuchadnezzar, was king and God written his destiny on the wall, what he was going to do?

Did you know that before your day start, it is written on the wall?

It is called ordinances of your day.

God has an ordinance of our day, and you better believe Satan has an ordinance of how he wants your day to go.

Sometimes I could be sleeping at night and when I opened my eyes, I could see what God want me to see in the spirit realm.

I saw a bunch of writing on my wall one night.

At first, I did not understand what that meant until God gave me the revelation about what I was seeing.

I would see a bunch of writing for a couple of seconds, then it would disappear.

The first writing I seen was graffiti on my wall.

God was teaching me about curses that Satan and his servant had placed on me for that day.

When I saw them, I had to break the curses that were sent to me in the night season.

God do not show us things just to show us.

He has a reason.

What is hidden in the dark?

God will bring to the light.

He will show you what Satan and his agents is doing against you and your family and others.

So, when God show you whether in a dream or a vision, we must pray against it.

Break all curses that are sent to us and command all demonic spirits associated with those curses to leave in Jesus's name.

# 25

## *Mason pt. 1*

Why don't we pray before we join any organizations?

We assume too much that something is of God just because a Bible is there.

Even if your mother or father has joined, we assume it's okay.

Masons, Eastern Stars, and Christians has been tricked out of their salvation, replacing it with the oath they made with the vow at initiation to the organization.

Example, knock

Who's there?

Man seeking light.

How are you in the dark if Christ is in you and if Christ is your light?

They submit into a horrible murder if they break the vow, committing themselves to have their ears slice off, their tongues split from tip to root, their heart rip out and place on a dungeon hill to rot, or their skulls smoke off and their brains exposed to the rays of the noon day sun.

Should they violate this oath?

Is this something that Christians with value will speak on themselves?

James 5:12 say, "Let your yes be yes and your no be no."

Life and death are in the power of the tongue.

Later, as you climb the ladder by going up to higher degrees, you start it with the Bible.

Then you have the book of the Quran.

Men cannot serve two masters.

You will loved one and hate the other.

This is something you cannot overlook.

Satan has had many years of practicing how to deceive us.

The Lord says you cannot defeat Satan and oppose his lies but through Jesus Christ when he brings what hidden to the light.

This gets better if a Mason commit a crime and is guilty when they go to court.

If the judge is a Mason and a lawyer, they make hand signs and say certain words that let the judge know who he is with the lawyer's help.

As court goes on, only Mason members in the courtroom know what taken place to get them off or flash their ring to get out of trouble if stopped by the police.

Why not trust God and rely on his mercy instead of man?

The truth should make you free.

If you want to be free, they are replacing God with their organization instead of trusting God, they trust their Mason members to do it for them.

Even with Job's connection, putting God out of everything and replacing him with something else.

For some of you who think about joining the Mason, let me share with you the secret that is waiting on you.

When you make it to the top, high levers, this lever is called adoption.

This is where Mason is brought into fellowship of Lucifer.

He is guided into swearing an oath and being yoked to the temple of Lucifer.

Unfortunately, he is led into making a pact with Lucifer.

This is basically selling of the soul to the devil.

Mason promised to surrender himself, body, soul, and spirit to Lucifer.

Usually promised to grant him all his worldly desires.

After the seven years are up, if he has been a good servant, Lucifer would give him another seven years.

If he fails, you know what time it is.

It's stated from an ex-Mason member, William Schnoebelen, on page 194 in his book, Mason's Beyond the Light.

All Christians should read this book.

William Schnoebelen stated that most Mason was blissfully in the dark about the light they have.

This is where the leaders want them.

They did not know the secret they were guarding so carefully.

Like workers in a classified project, they were only allowed to know as much as they need to know to work in the system.

These poor men, many of them were churchgoers, was ignorant of the big picture.

They would be applauded to learn the truth, concealed behind the layers of the allegory.

# 26

## *Mason pt. 2*

William Schnoebelen was an ex-Mason that got into the highest level in masonry

He had gotten in levels that most masons do not know exists, but thanks to a Christian lady that God had used to pray him out of the organization and now he is exposing the lie about the Mason that it is not a Christian organization at all.

He had made it to the top, so he knows what he is talking about, and he want to help others know the truth before they join and if they already join, he is telling them especially Christians to get out.

The people they are under is sworn to secrecy and will not reveal the things before its time and most of them do not know much the ones that know are on higher levels.

They are not going to tell you until you reach the top and do the certain rituals then Satan himself would appear and offer them wealth and power by selling their soul to him.

The reason why I wrote about this organization is because my first husband was thinking about joining and as he was telling me about it all of it I felt a dark presence about it so I pray about it and ask the Lord to reveal to me the truth about this organization that my husband at the time and family was connected to so Bobby thought that since his family was a part of it he should too.

I did some research on it and find out what other ex-Mason had to say about it that later gave their life to the Lord.

One night my co-worker and I was talking at work and the subject came up and I was sharing with her something I had found out as we were talking, and a member overheard our conversation and told us that we better shut up and do not talk about that subject because there are people that will harm us and kill to protect the Mason name.

I look at him and told him that no weapon form against me shall prosper.

Soon as the guy had a chance to inform some of his Mason buddies, they attacked me at home while in my bed.

The next night and a man came in my room in the spirit and told me to shut up about the Masons and do not read no more information about them.

All sudden this evil force started beating me up in my face with little, tiny pebbles and I say out loud in the name of Jesus go and they left.

All they did was prove my point that the Mason members is practicing witchcraft they are witches and warlocks they are train on how to Astro project to use their spirits bodies to travel in the spirits realms

If I could do the research and God revealed to me the truth, why cannot others do the same no matter if their mothers or father is in it.

This is the catch.

If you join this demonic organization the spirit that is over the Mason organization have the rights to blind the minds of everybody that joins.

That means once you join the dark things that you do, and practice does not seem wrong.

In the Bible the scripture said the God of this world has blind the minds of the people.

In 2nd Chronicles 4:4 Christians are blinded once they join.

Here are the names of the Mason members who wrote most of the literature that the Mason used in most of their meetings.

Here is a note from Adam Weishaupt who was a Satanist stated he bragged it.

In a letter he wrote and say how he would suddenly destroy Christians by using deception for those who fell for his poly.

Another Masonic member named Baron Vonknigge

I have put meaning to all those dark symbols and have prepared both degrees introducing beautiful ceremonies which I have selected from those of ancient communions.

Combine it with these on rosaica masonry and hence

JD Buck, a Mason, explained the most profound secrets of the Mason are not revered in the lodge at all they belong to the few.

In other words, the rituals that they are doing in their lodges is an evil practice.

They tell them it means something else, but the true knowledge of the symbols and rituals are dark practices of witchcraft that are hidden from them all except the people at the top of the pyramid

They know the truth.

Albert Pike and earlier Mason from the beginning wrote a book called Irano-Aryan faith and doctrine as contaminated in the Zen Avest

He stated that he took all obligations to white men not Negroes as brethren.

We will leave the Masonry

Albert Pike is the founder of the Ku Klux Klan.

A lot of these earlier pioneers were Satanists.

# 27

## *Mason pt. 3*

There are enough problems in the world.

Why add to it by involving ourselves in organizations or clubs that we know nothing about or done any kind of research on it?

Just because we want to be a part of something that sounds good or because someone is in it that we look up to.

Sometimes we hook up with things that hurt us and our families on the end, physically and spiritually.

It started in the garden when Satan deceived Adam and Eve stating that you will be as God's.

Men always had a thirst for knowledge and power

But only to find out that in the Mason that the illumination light is wisdom from Satan and knowledge.

Money and power are all coming from him.

But at what cost?

1 Corinthians 10:21 Ye cannot drink the cup of the Lord and the cup of devils.

Ye cannot be partakers of the Lord's table and of the table of the devils.

Did you know that in the organization of the Shriner 2% of the money raised go to the children's hospital to country clubs where they throw wild parties with a lot of drinking and orgies going on by the expense of the donations.

Satan hides this well.

The Shriner have an Islamic connection?

The real name of the Shriner is called Ancient Arabic Order, Nobler of the Mystical Shriner

It is a demonic Islam religion.

When Shriner do initiation, they must swear the oath on the book of the Quran.

They stated, "May Allah, the God of Arabic Moslem and Mohammed, the God of our Father, suppose, me to the entire fulfillment of the same Amen."

The Shriners is swearing in the name of Allah and calling Allah his God.

Muslims deny the identity of Jesus Christ and his resurrection.

Christians, do you know what the red Fez symbol on the Shriner hat stands for?

The red and gold colors with the sword.

It is said that the entire Moroccan Muslims, its color is from the fact that centuries ago Islamic armies invaded Fez and slaughtered thousands of Christians who resides there.

The blood of the Christians' mortars ran in the streets and the Islamic holy warriors dipped their headgear in the blood and dyed them scarlet.

The Fez is a commemoration of the murder of thousands of Christians.

No wonder Satan smiles when Christian wear proudly stated by an ex-Mason member named William Schnoebelen

Please buy his book about Masons.

You really need to read what's inside so the truth shall set you free.

I am not talking to unsaved people in this organization.

I am talking to Christians.

Be contempt to be a part of your own organization as a Christian in your church, not a part of somebody else's organization with rituals and oath and gnostic teaching that is against your Creator God.

# 28

## *Tattoos*

Leviticus 19:28 Did you know why God said you shall not make any cutting in your flesh for the dead, nor print any marks upon you?

I am the Lord.

First King 18:28 When you cut yourself on purpose for a tattoo, writing, there is bloodshed in that you can or might not see taking place.

When the people in the Bible days cut themselves, they did it to draw demons to them for a purpose, to do something for them.

The demon will show up to make your wish happen, which is witchcraft.

Before I can go any further, I must explain to you the real meaning of witchcraft.

Witchcraft is when you are dealing with the supernatural.

For instance, you will summon the demon to come to you to get something done that you cannot do naturally.

Let's get real, there is two kingdoms in this world, God's kingdom and Satan's kingdom.

If you pray to God to get something done, he will send his angels out for your favor.

But if you serve Satan, you are going about getting things the wrong way through demonic spirits to go and manipulate people's minds by demonic forces in the invisible realm.

People who are in the occult know for a fact that demons are real and it's affecting almost everyone in some kind of way.

But some Christians don't believe that demons can affect them, but when you lack knowledge about them, they can.

My people perish because of the lack of knowledge in Hosea 4:6.

I know that most people do not believe in witchcraft because I heard so many people say it.

If you do not believe that witchcraft is real, how can you believe in the Bible because it is in there.

Let God, word be true and every man a liar.

How can you fight against something that you don't believe in?

when witchcraft comes to your home, they will call it something else other than what it is.

Going back to the topic, if you cut yourself on purpose for a tattoo or any kind of mark, whether your children name or Jesus's name, it is still wrong.

God told you no in Leviticus 19:.28 because you are in ignorance of what you are doing.

You do not know the spiritual effects behind it.

If you cut yourself for accident, the demon does not move to your aid because you did not do it on purpose.

Satan knows that he could not get this generation to cut themselves on purpose, so he came up with tattoos.

If you get a tattoo, your flesh is cut to burn that mark in your skin for life.

when the flesh is cut, demons come to them in the spirit realm.

They now have legal rights to affect them in many ways.

Once you get one tattoo, you will desire more.

Satan do not want parts of you, he wants to cover you up from head to toe.

If your body is covered with tattoos from head to toe, who will you look like God or Satan?

Lucifer just tricked you to get a permanent mark on your body for life, all in the name of fashion which is graffiti.

That's why God tells us not to do things in the Bible to protect us because it will have spiritual effects on us that we cannot see naturally or understand when strange things start to happen.

Anytime we disobey God, it will always have consequences whether we realize it or not.

If you ever come to the knowledge of the truth about tattoos, you can ask God to forgive you in the name of Jesus and he will.

# 29

## *Women in Ministry*

This chapter is talking about women in ministry.

I feel like I need to clear up some wrong kind of thinking when it comes to women preachers.

It is not about gender.

That is what Satan used to put stumbling blocks in front of women by using most men to do it.

There are religious spirits that work through men stating that nobody can do this except I

Do you know who this spirit sounds like?

The Pharisees and the Sadducees

Who were teachers of the law at that time trying to stop the disciples from carrying out the ministry of God.

Thinking that they are special, and they are the only one who qualifies to do it.

Don't think too highly of yourself than you ought to.

God can use any vessel that he chooses.

It is not up to man.

God does not need their permission.

If God did not want a woman to preach, he would never fill her with the Holy Spirit.

The Holy Spirit is the one who preaches and teaches through men and women.

The Holy Spirit hears what God is saying and he tells them what God wants them to know and what to tell the people.

The Holy Spirit uses Christians as a vessel to carry out the purpose of God.

The Holy Spirit was sent down here from God to dwell in the Believers

Let me explain the function of the Holy Spirit.

He gives us gifts as he will.

Speaking' in tongues, interpretation in tongues, discerning of Spirits healing, prophecy, miracles, administration, gifts and Words and wisdom.

of knowledge.

Ephesians 4:11 He gives some to be apostles, prophets, evangelists, pastors, and teachers for the perfecting of the saints, for the work of the ministry, for edifying of the body of Christ.

Anytime we get in the flesh, we always mess it up.

Men and women make up the body of Christ and we cannot say we don't need one another.

Stop looking at our differences and look at our togetherness.

In Galatians 3:28, there are no Jew or Gentiles, no male or female.

We are all one in Jesus Christ.

Keep this in mind.

The Holy Spirit is the ministry.

He is hearing from God, telling preachers what to say and when someone get healed, the Holy Spirit is the healer etc.

Father God is using the Holy Spirits to bring glory from heaven to here on earth.

Let go and let God.

Let's stop fighting' one another when we work for the same team

The only thing that is different from men and women, preachers, is their sex, which is not needed to work in God's kingdom.

God is a spirit, and the Bible is spiritual.

In the realm of the spirit, there are no boundaries and there is no limitation in God.

But anytime we start looking in the flesh, it always hinders the work of God.

Let's get out of the flesh today and get into the realm of the spirit with endless possibilities.

# 30

## *Church Titles*

I must shed some light on the devil patterns he had been using on almost all Christians.

Church leaders by using their own titles of their ministry to keep Christians separated like Apostolic, Pentecostal, Holiness Baptist, Methodist etc. creating a system and a role on how each church functions and if they do not function the way they think each one will, they will not visit their church only their own kind.

Does each church member believe in the doctrines of the Holy Bible?

Do they teach from the same Bible?

If so, then what is the problem?

Most pastors don't recognize how the enemy has influenced them throughout history.

The devil knows that God moves quicker in numbers.

That's why he tries so hard to keep them focusing on their differences and not their togetherness.

Can you imagine if these churches would drop their titles and get on one accord by letting the Holy Spirit lead them on what to pray for?

This world would change instantly.

The devil knows that very well.

I have noticed that when I go to church conferences out of town that people will come from all around the world, and nobody cares about which church or domination you come from because most of them were on one accord with Jesus Christ.

That is why I believe so many people got healed and delivered from their problems because nothing was separating them from getting their breakthrough unlike their own ministry by hindering the Holy Spirit from being used, replacing him with man rules.

Demonic spirits minister to some Christian minds so they would accept their thoughts as their own.

To keep the power of God out of the church, we as Christians have the power to change the world by God if we could only get past our differences.

But if we believe that our way is the only way, then a change will not come.

# 31

## *Jehovah Witness*

I want to discuss false teaching by Jehovah Witness they believe that after Jesus Christ death on the cross he gave all the power back to the Father which is false and

When it comes down to the knowledge of the function of the Holy Spirit, they don't believe the truth about the third trinity

Jehovah Witness don't believe in the gifts of the Holy Spirit especially speaking in tongues.

They believe that the Holy Spirit power has ceased.

They also believe that the Holy Spirit power is from the devil.

When Jesus died on the cross in Matthew 12:31, the Lord says that He will forgive anyone except blasphemy of the Holy Ghost.

You cannot call the Holy Spirit power, a devil.

You must be very careful of the words we speak.

When Jesus was casting out demons, the scribes said that He was casting out demons by the power of the prince, of Beelzebub

Jesus told them how could Satan cast out Satan?

A house divide can't stand.

Luke 11:18, Jehovah Witness lost their power when they did not rightfully believe in the power of the Holy Spirit has in a Christian life, including laying hands on the sick so the sick will recover, casting out demons, speaking in tongues, word of wisdom, word of prophecy, etc.

Jehovah Witness believes there is no more prophets today based on Psalm 74:9 which reads, "We do not see our signs there is no more prophets, nor is there any among us who knows how long."

If there were no more prophets, God would be contradicting Himself because in Ephesians 4:1, He gave some apostles, some prophets, some evangelists, and some teachers and preachers, prophets of old, when they prophesied, the Holy Spirit came on the outside of them.

Now the Holy Spirit is on the inside of believers.

After Jesus died on the cross, He said, "You will receive power from high because I have gone to the Father.

You will be able to do greater works."

Acts 1:18, what Jehovah Witness got to realize is the Holy Spirit is the ministry.

He is the preacher.

He is the teacher.

He is the healer, etc.

Without Him, you will only have the flesh which profits, nothing but flesh.

What Satan has done to Jehovah Witness is he stole their power by tricking them to believe that the Holy Spirit power is from Him.

Hindering them from being healed and delivered by Jesus Christ and from the operation in the fullness power of God, they have no spiritual power only working from the flesh, the doctrine of man, the letter kills, but it is the Spirit that gives life.

2 Corinthians 3:6.

# 32

## *Depopulation*

I read an article by Jimmy Carter that state that the government wants to depopulate the earth by 2025.

The report was called Global 2000.

I can believe that because if we look at the food situation today it's full of hormones and chemicals and metals which is harmful to us all.

I believe that we're most cancer is coming from.

A lot of doctors are prescribing a lot of medicine that do not work, that sometimes make the patient's symptoms worse, or they lose their life, and some doctors are not held accountable.

What about the heinous abortion clinic in Philadelphia that was run by Dr.

Kermitt Korsnell that had murder so many babies a day which were supported by the government at the time.

Babies that were born alive at this clinic.

This evil doctor will take his instrument and spit the baby neck to enforce the death.

Some of the baby body parts were stored in jars in this clinic.

People in the community had known for years about this doctor and what was taking place at his clinic.

They got the local authorities to investigate at the time when they had fine bad things going on they did nothing about it so they went to a higher authority and found out that the Department of Health top official recounted a meeting under the new administration governor of Philadelphia at that time had decided that if they investigate the clinic they would find a lot of violations and that would keep women from having abortions.

Sounds like the depopulation to me because in the future the less people the more the government can control under the new world order.

When I was growing up in the 70s and 80s there was a lot of baby commercials to sell diapers.

Now we see today a lot of dogs and cat commercials that is dominating the TV right now.

The point our government is showing America is to get a pet instead of a child.

# 33

## *Win Worley*

In this pamphlet book by Win Worley called Doctors, Demon, and Medicine.

He talks about the real meaning of medicine and physicians is to cure, heal, or recover completely.

Satan has reversed these meanings in Matthew 5:34,37.

Forbids, us from swearing are taken oath to false gods.

The oath that doctors make when they swear in sounds good, but it is a curse from God the Father Himself.

They start their oath with "I" swear by Apollo, the physician and the Aesculapius and all the gods and goddesses.

The word Apollyon in Revelation 9:11 comes from the same root as Apollo.

He is the God of destruction, medicine, archery prophecy, music, poetry, and the highest type of masculine beauty.

Aesculapius is the God of medicine, the son of Apollo by a demon Nymph

All gods and goddesses, the caduceus is the staff of Mercury, twined by two serpents, gods of commerce, messenger of the gods, cleverness, lying thievery, eloquence, travel, etc.

Satan plans the sickness, then programs the symptoms which are treated by sincere and duty-bound doctors.

Because of this, a believer should break any evil soul tied with "satanic medicine" and pray much about use of such things.

Read the PDR listing all current prescription drugs and side effects.

The word medicine occurs in Proverbs 17-22, Jeremiah 30-13, 46-11, and Ezekiel 47-12.

The root word is Gehah" = to remove or heal.

Teruwthah" = to remedy.

"Rapha" = to heal.

The word means a complete cure.

The word physician is used five times in the Bible.

The Hebrew root word is "Rapha" meaning to stitch restore, make, hold, heal thoroughly.

The God of this world, Satan has introduced into medicine a group of chemicals and drugs, spells, relief, relievers, tranquilizers, uppers, downers etc.

These are prescribed and are on the shelf.

We are told that they are safe to use or else they will not be on the shelf.

That is not necessarily true.

Such drugs and chemicals in the Bible are associated with sorcery, the Greek, Pharmakia medicine, pharmacy, magicians, sorcery, prisoner.

The use of chemicals by sorcery in the Bible made it easy for the users to be invaded by evil spirits.

Scriptures on sorcery is Acts 8:9 and Revelation 9:21- 18:23.

Notice the real definition of medicine in the Bible states, "Real medicine heals or cures."

Our problem arose when Satan calls world scientists, researchers, and medicine professionals to endorse pain-reliever drugs which have no curative value.

What about mind-altering drugs and chemicals?

Some church members will condemn alcohol as a reliever, yet if the doctors prescribe valium or Liberin, they will take it.

Satan calls aches and pains and agony diseases which affect the mind and will emotions.

Reliever drugs do not cure mask the symptoms.

Some pain relievers are so powerful that it will come against the Holy Spirit and cause a barrier between them.

Tranquilizers can separate a person's mind from reality.

Tranquilizers is a witchcraft drug, regardless of who prescribes it.

Any person who takes it is under a curse from God Himself because it is sorcery.

Witchcraft is open doors for evil spirits to come in just like hypnosis, transcendental meditation and yoga.

Many mental institutions woefully give inmates tranquilizers daily and parents give their children drugs because of hypoactive so they can control them.

Very few follow scriptures and motivations to do the work of Jesus in deliverance, but chemicals controllers are "administrated" instead.

# 34

## *Aliens*

In 2012, I was working as a security guard in my hometown at a plant.

I was working the midnight shift by myself.

Nobody was in the plant because all the plant workers left by 2 a.m.

The sightings happened around 4 a.m.

I was in the guard house, and I had wanted a snack, so I went inside of the plant where the vending machine were as I was leaving out of the building.

I saw in the sky a bunch of buildings attached to one another with lots of tiny lights around it.

It looked like Star Trek the next generation.

The object flew across my head slowly.

I didn't know what to do to run or stay still so I just watched it until it left out of my sight.

I was praying to the Lord and binding up any evil spirits that trying to communicate with me in any fashion that would cause me harm.

Warning to anyone, if you do come across them, guard your mind, do not let them talk to you.

It will cause you problems later.

I don't know why I saw that spacecraft and other sightings.

Aliens is fallen angels.

You have Greys and you have a Nordic.

The Nordic look like human and they can shift shape

The Grays are mixed with experiment

That's why some of them look weird.

Christians, we do have power and authority over them in Jesus's name.

# 35

## *Gun Control*

In the book of the Bible in Joel 1:7, God asked Satan, "Where do you come from?"

He replied, "Go into and from this earth and walk back and forth on it."

Satan was seeking who he can devour.

Some people who carry guns, I believe, don't just wake up and say that they want to kill a bunch of people.

Satan and his demons seek out people whose mind is in the right condition for them to place their evil thoughts and ideals in their mind to destroy people.

Some people in the government and other evil organizations are in the cult and can communicate with Satan and his demons fallen angels to carry out the devil's plan in this world.

Technology can send silent sound waves related to EM/RF technology to affect people.

Mental stability, their moods, their emotions, they can send evil wave forms to call depression to innocent people.

This is what I call evil technology.

# 36

## *Satanist on Assignment*

While in the process of writing this book, I had to take a break because warfare had gotten so heavy that most of my attention had to be on whatever I was going through and how to stop it.

I was surprised when the Lord have revealed to me about something that was taking me out of the window at night when I was a child.

He had revered to me what had happened to me.

He says my family, my bloodline had dedicated me to Satan.

when I was taken out through the window, during those times they was doing rituals on me, they were putting things inside of my body so I can work for Satan's kingdom.

Now, all things had started to make sense to me as to what I was going through.

I found out that I had trackers inside of me, and other evil devices inside of my body, including my head.

I had no clue that all of this was on the inside of me growing up, until things start to happen to me later in life.

It started when I start working at this plant.

We got a new supervisor that I found out later that he was a high-level Satanist.

Mason.

When I first saw him, I felt like he was probably on assignment against me, because the way he had looked at me, his looks was like he was up to something, but I had no clue of the amount of suffering that I was about to face.

One day, I took sick at work.

I was going to my car to go home, and out of no way he touched my forehead.

He starts mumbling and saying some things, I got in my vehicle, not realizing what had just taken place because I was feeling bad my defenses was down.

I went home end up going to the emergency room what was going on with me was demonic and it didn't show up on the machine

I found out that this is how Satan got back at me, for not carrying out the demonic call on my life that my family had initiated

Even though I did not know of it, I had no clue that I was dedicated to Satan.

I didn't know I was really programmed as a child.

When he touched me, he had activated me to the demonic realm

Now, these evil forces and beings could touch me physically and spiritually, and I could be torment and punish.

I start seeing light portals coming out of the walls ceiling floors windows with evil being came through

I was attacked at night, spirits coming in to snatch my heart out of my chest.

I had things moving around in my stomach.

I was frightened by these evil beings that come in and torment me

I was being attacked by fallen angels, spirit guides witches, warlocks, dead human spirits aliens demons, trying to take my organs out of my body, trying to kill me.

Oh my God.

I prayed to the Lord in pain for all of this to stop.

[Noted] God tell us in his word,1 Timothy 5:22 don't be quick to let someone to lay hands on you and in Ecclesiastes, 10:8 if you break an edge the serpent will bite you our body has gates."

When the wrong person touches you, they could be transferring spirits to you, they could be opening you up for demonic things.

But I got more than a bite.

I quit that job.

there are so many people out here, SRA is unknown to most in the world.

Innocent people are being killed, put in asylum.

Most people don't even believe this exist

The occult just gets away with a lot of things because this is hidden

I heard a lot of people say that they don't believe in witchcraft, even though it's in the Bible.

God talk about witches and sorcery, divination, etc.

what they are doing is calling God a liar.

But God's scripture says, "Let God's word be true."

Every man is a liar, Romans 3:6

He says also, "My people perish because of lack of knowledge.

Hosea 4:6

# 37

## *Stolen Birthrights*

If some of you wondering why you was having a hard time in life and cannot seem to be successful at the things you do, it might be because your family, your bloodline, ancestors sold your birthright.

This could even be done before you are born.

Your family can sell your birthright by trading on their bloodline for money, good services, promotion, positions, fame, fortune, property, etc.

They can even dedicate you to Satan without your permission because most of the time you are a baby or might not even be born yet.

Some people sold their entire bloodline out to the demonic.

So many people would not be aware of this.

How could you pray against something that you don't know anything about?

Until now, you must do a bloodline cleansing, repentance to get free.

# 38

## *Pagan Holidays*

Constantine was the Roman Emperor of the Roman Catholic Church.

He had removed a lot of information from the Bible.

They did not want future generations to know.

They mixed holidays with pagan deities for the world to worship them out of ignorance.

They took something from the Bible and mixed it with paganism.

For instance, Christmas, the 25th is Nimrod birthday, not Jesus Christ.

Once you put that Christmas tree into your house you are practicing tree worship

Satan don't care how he gets you to practice idolatry

He knows he must dress it up to make it look good in your eyes.

If a Christmas tree is in your house, it is tree worship.

Eve ate the fruit off the tree one time, but now you worship that tree in the month of December, every year when you bend down to put presents under it you are making homage.

# 39

## *Spirit Spouse*

For some of you who are not married, did you ever wonder why you can't seem to find the right one to marry?

The reason why you are not married is because you are already married in the spirit.

You might have a spirit spouse.

They claim you as theirs.

What had happened is your ancestors have made covenants with water spirits in exchange for something they want.

That's how they have gotten into the bloodline because of an evil trade.

For some of you that is going through this, you will have a dream of having sex with someone

Every time you sleep with them in your dreams, you are renewing the covenant.

Whether you know it or not, there will be times when you are up for a promotion or something big and good is about to happen for you.

You will go to sleep.

Next thing you notice, you will be having sex with someone in your dreams

Once you do that your blessing is cancel

God will hold you accountable as if you are really sleeping with that person.

Even though it's in the spirit you are having spiritually sex

what you must do is break the evil covenant contracts, the oath, and vows, evil agreements that were made by your ancestors.

In Exodus 34:7, when your parents' ancestors' sin, your children, children, children reap the consequences for the sin.

But until someone repents for it, it will stop.

I know that most Christians think that they are only responsible for the sins that they do.

You must repent for your family, your ancestors' sins that open evil doors in the bloodline.

In church, we are taught to repent for our sins only

There is a need for bloodline repentance, especially in the black African American churches.

A lot of people think that whites are stopping them from being successful.

No, it's not the whites.

It's your bloodline that made covenants with Satan against you for something that they thought was more important at the time.

A lot of people even today are doing evil trading on their bloodline.

Satan only comes to steal, kill, and destroy.

I can remember when I was fasting and praying, and I couldn't understand why at a certain time I would fall asleep, and some man would be on top of me having sex.

And I had prayed for this to stop.

Once I became conscious in my sleep what was going on, I prayed to God to stop it.

And I got so upset, with God, because I was telling him, "Why is this keep happening to me?

This is not right.

Why don't you stop this?"

It took a while to get rid of that spirit spouse, but God did it.

He delivers me, and I was so glad when He did.

It's not right for anyone to be sleeping with you while you are sleeping.

That's a curse, and you need to break it.

# 40

## *Facebook*

Almost everyone has a Facebook page where they can connect with people all around the world.

It can be a good thing, or it can be a bad thing.

Let me tell you why.

You have all those contacts with people you know and don't know.

Let's talk about the ones you don't know.

But this is for Christians only.

Christians who accept a friend's request and don't know them.

You look on their pages and you will see all kind of scriptures or Godly things all over their page.

you think they are Christians like you.

And you think that they are positive people like you.

But some of them are witches and warlocks

Once you accept their friend's request, you just became their friends.

You just enter into an evil agreement with them.

So now he or she has legal rights on you.

They can send you curses, spells, vexes hexes coming into your life, coming into your house and dreams.

They can bring illness.

They know who you are, but you do not know them.

they are coming against you in the spirit first, then in the natural.

Your life just got harder, and you don't know why.

You didn't ask Father God.

You just assumed that Facebook was play and fun.

Facebook can be used for good and evil.

The dark kingdom knows this better than us.

# 41

## *Fallen Angels, Giants*

When you read the Bible in Genesis 6, it talks about the sons of God mating with the women.

That had created giants in the land.

God was so upset with them that He had cause a flood in Noah time.

But still after the flood, some still survived.

We know this because of Joshua and his army fought and defeat them by the Lord.

David killed Goliath by a rock and a slain in 1Samuel 17:49.

The fallen sons of God not only created giants, but they also mated with animals, reptiles, fishes, and other underwater creatures.

That how mermaids came to be

And half man, half woman, with animal's parts a man head with a horse body Levithan, Behemoth, the dragon, the monsters, the beasts, etc.

The fallen angels could shift shape.

they have the power to change their spirit body.

In Jude 1:6, the angels, which not kept their first estate, but left their own habitation, He has reserved them in everlasting chains, under darkness, into judgment of the great day.

Archaeologists found a lot of remains from giants.

You can see the big bones they dig up.

There are pictures on the internet and other platforms.

The fallen angels and giant are here, believe it or not.

Occultists, witches, and warlocks, movie stars, movie producers, our high-level government bankers, politicians, artists, contact them to gain information and knowledge for power in their position.

Witches learn how to do certain spells, hexes, and vexes for their craft.

Some Bankers and people in the financial institution learn how to make more money and to get in higher level positions.

Movie producers get movies ideas from them, artists get music and other ideas to advance in their profession.

Politicians gain information even to win election.

In other words, for them to get anything from them.

They must worship them.

They do blood sacrifices, rituals, drink, concoction they make covenants contracts vows oath evil agreements to them etc.

They are spiritual beings who want to be worshipped, like Satan.

In Isaiah 14:13, I will build my throne above the stars.

The fallen angels wanted to be worshipped just like God, so they would make trades for them to worship them the people that connected to them had sold their souls for money wealth power and goods their third eye is open so they can see them spiritually to communicate.

# 42

## *Artificial Intelligences*

>> Artificial intelligence Aliens technology with evil beasts, computers, and cell phones, is the type of system that was attacking me.

Through high power, frequency, wave, technology in the atmosphere.

This technology is from Satan's kingdom.

Fallen angels that fell with Satan taught man demonic knowledge and secret technology.

Evil science, among a lot of things.

Remember, these beings were once with God, the Father.

The angels that had learned from Father God, they know a lot of things.

most of all our technology and inventions today comes from them in an exchange for something.

There were trades, that were made among man, fallen angels, and other spiritual beings.

Some people do rituals, evil sacrifice to be able to communicate with demonic spirits

They sold their souls for money, wealth, and power.

I find myself being target by this system.

I am tracked, followed by occultist evil agents by the dark government.

The dark government has a payroll that they use to pay people to follow you around and blast evil frequencies into your body.

They would send evil frequencies heat waves technology to my head, that was off the charts

There were frequencies sent to my stomach and heart that felt awful.

This was pure torment.

This had gone on for years and I would beg

Father God how to stop this.

I came across a ministry that helps people like me I am still going through deliverance today

The metals content in my body came from foods I ate had help the

evil frequencies to torment me even stronger

There are dark electric magnetics is being used against us all in US

Enough metals in your body can cause health problems.

Why does the food and drug administration allow so many mentals in our food I believe it is because the people behind the New World Orders is controlling the world.

The Beast system is already showing us its ugly head.

If you are paying attention, it is in our faces believe it or not.

5G, 6G, 7G, 8G, 9G is very dangerous for our bodies.

Why did the smart TVs come out in the first place?

Our government told us we had to get digital boxes, then we purchased the smart TVs, the old television is the thing of the past.

Technology is not always good technologies.

All these signals in our airway around us, there is more to the television, cell phones, computers than we think.

We are going to find out in depths of this soon.

The Lord has shown me in my dreams that we are being watched through our television, in our homes also can you imagine in the future when people start to purchase more robots, and they think that they are computer program but are entities inside.

# 43

## *Not Humans*

There are aliens, mermaids, and other beings that are walking around among us every day.

And you don't know it.

You do not know who they are because they look like us.

I have encounters with some of them and there are others that I cannot describe them to you because I don't have the name for them.

Mermaids can shapeshift into half woman, half men, and have the body of a fish.

There are movies on this, and they are hoping that you don't believe it.

There is going to come a time when the Lord is going to expose them all and you will be shocked when you find out that the man or woman you marry is not human.

Whenever that time comes, some people would already be aware of them, but most will not

Watch as well as pray.

When I was in school, they taught us that Greek, Roman, Egyptian mythology creatures did not exist because it could not be proven by science.

We must understand that the planet Earth was here before we were.

lots of those creatures was here and is here now.

Just in the spirit realm, just like the other spiritual beings, for God and Satan to get anything done here on Earth, they must use humans.

When I got saved, Father God, Jesus Christ, Holy Spirit came into my life and everyone else God wanted to use to carry out his kingdom business here on Earth.

When humans commit to Satan by selling their soul, they open their door to Lucifer, Satan, demons, fallen angels, dead human spirits, Aliens and others mythological creatures to come into their life to help them carry out Satan's business here on Earth.

We invite them from their dimensions to ours.

We open the spiritual doors to them, and they will come in, believe it or not.

# 44

## *Occult Workers*

Whenever a loved one is in the hospital, make sure someone stays with them.

Some doctors, nurses, nurse assistants, and other hospital workers and ambulance drivers could be in the occult.

when Satan tells a doctor, "I need this many souls," what do you think will happen to your loved ones?

Your loved ones could die for no reason at all because of them.

you must be with your loved ones and pray.

Everybody who has a degree in any field might not gotten it fair.

They could have made an evil covenant with Satan to get it.

Think about that.

# 45

## *Dead Human Spirits*

In the book of 2 Corinthians 5:8 most Christians quote this scripture when it comes to the dead absent from the body present with the lord Satan hope you don't get what I'm about to expose because this is his weapon he was using against mankind for centuries, that you will not believe that when humans passed away, they still have a will."

When Paul passed away, he went up to internal life. With the lord

But for some who sold their soul to the devil, and for some who don't know the Lord, and others who want revenge on the person who had killed them, will not go through the silver channel when they pass away.

when the silver channel closes, you are stuck here on earth until Judgment Day.

they will roam the earth until the end of the world comes in the spirit realm.

There are some who were supposed to go to heaven, they didn't leave because they wanted to be with their loved ones.

some people could feel the presence of the loved one that had passed because they are close with them.

you can talk to your loved ones and tell them that you are okay

Ask Father God to send his escort angels to escort them into an internal life.

God will honor that.

I had experience that for myself after a loved one passed, I could feel their presence.

And I asked the Lord to send his angels and escort them to internal life.

I didn't know the name of the channel until years later.

I came across some ministries that known about dead spirits roaming the earth and effecting people

A lot of deliverance ministries have closed during the past because they were burnt out.

Because they were commanding demons to leave the person, but it was dead human spirit instead you do not have authority over them in Jesus' name, but you do have authority over demons in the name of Jesus Christ.

I can remember reading the Bible when I first got saved.

And I came across the scriptures about demonic spirits unclean spirits and evil spirits.

But then to me, it was not specific as clarity to me at the time.

We just assume that unclean spirits were demons, and evil spirits but I lean that the unclean spirits are dead human spirits.

When I was a little child, there had come a time I could remember a lot of deaths were occurring and I asked my grandmother, where does people go when they die?

She told me that everyone doesn't go up to heaven or hell.

Some people would roam the earth until Judgement Day.

I believe Father God had told me to ask her that because I was going to experience dead human spirits later in life

I always had remembered what she had said, and it always has stuck to my mind.

My grandmother was a high-level witch.

That's why she knows those things.

Witches work with Satan, dead human spirits, fallen angels, giants, demons, aliens, etc.

So, they know what's going on.

Death covenants can be made to Satan in the book of Isaiah 28:18.

It states that your covenant with death shall be annulled your agreement with hell shall not stand

If death covenants cannot be made, why would he say it in the first place?

ancestors' family members can make death covenants against their bloodline. Without their permission

After they die, they could use that family member in their bloodline to live inside of their body after they die.

And when that family member died, they go to the next one.

I could give you an example.

They can roam the earth until they wanted to rest, they will use their family member's body.

To be their house.

most people don't give them permission in the first place it was their bloodline that open the doors to this

Most of them cause pain and in your body.

That what had happened to me when this family member passed, I started to have pain in certain parts of my body.

That was so awful.

I seek the Lord, and he told me what happened.

And I was on my road to deliverance since then.

I must warn you that they are some of the stubborn spirits you will encounter.

be prepared to fight your way to freedom.

They don't want to give up their house.

it's very important to do bloodline repentance, especially if you have witches in your bloodline.

In Deuteronomy 18:10, 12 states, "There shall not be found among you anyone that makes his or her son or daughter to pass through the fire or use divination or observe by the time

117

or an enchanter or witch or a shaman or a consultative with the medium witch or wizard or a necromancer.

Necromancer is a person who communicates with the dead.

If the dead is in heaven or hell, how are they communicating with them?

Because they never went up to eternity.

They are here in the spirit realm roaming around us until Judgment Day to get rid of the bondage.

We must put the axe at the root of the tree.

# 46

## *Closing*

The devil only comes to kill steal and destroy.

He cannot be everywhere at one time like Jesus.

he must use his servants in the place of him.

On your jobs, in your neighborhood, in your churches, at your restaurants, at the hospitals, at gas station at grocery stores etc.

Everywhere you go his workers are there.

You cannot see them because they blend in like camouflage.

They know more about you than you know about them.

They are always on assignment against God's children.

Their third eyes open through Satanism.

When you go to the restaurant, bless your food.

Some of them will come on your jobs on assignment to get closer to you.

And once you trust them, they will turn your life upside down.

And you never expect it was them because they will try their best to do almost everything for you that you asked them to do.

So, you can trust them

In the churches witches and warlocks will try to get close to the pastor because if the pastor trusts them, they can do a lot of damage.

One of the easiest ways is in finances by being a good tither and a good giver. whenever the Lord shows the pastor, the person, that pastor would doubt it because of the generous giving once they get that pastor to trust them, that church is open gain.

The gifts of the spirit that God gave the church is not in use.

Most church members that speaking in tongues have no interpretation, they have some prophecy, no discernment spiritual but naturally

God gave these gifts to help bring in heaven on earth into the churches.

Most ministries don't used all the spiritual gifts just tongues and prophecy we disobey God that's why the body of Christ has no power just a good sounding sermon that make you feel good pay you're offering and start all over again next week nothing changed in your life

When I first received one of the gifts from the Lord which was discernment, it was like a nightmare at first.

I was seeing a lot of demonic things, a lot of demonic spirits.

I could feel them, I could be in a grocery store, I could feel spirits on certain parts of my body which had meanings.

what happened, I was discerning the people spirits around me.

I had started seeing witches and warlords in the church and then I say why can't the pastor see them?

Then once they know that I know who they were, it was war. they start sending me curses through the service and I could feel the spirits.

I could feel their spiritual weapons against my spiritual body.

But God was allowing this.

eventually I left I am not going to be in a place where the leaders don't believe that they are in their churches

No matter what church I've been to or wherever I went, there were always witches and warlocks there.

They are teaching Sunday school, Bible school

They at the door greeting people

There are singing on the choir.

There are on the treasurer committee in the church

I met many preachers that were witches and warlocks what a shame right under our nose.

I started to attend another ministry difference church same scenario

I went to bed one night after service

All the women that were witches at that church was all around my bed.

I say Father

I'm going to take a leave of absent from church right now.

Because most of the time I told the pastors, and they didn't believe me because

They were the people that they had counted on and was close to them

And who was I?

They were the yes men and yes women to them

Another thing I must bring up in churches that I see.

Ministers would tell their congregation to shake the hands of your neighbor beside you or to hug them.

The Lord taught me this.

He said when you shake someone's hand or hug them if they're witch you are coming into agreement with what they want to do to you.

most people would think it's friendly just to check a hand and to hug them you just gave them legal rights to curse you and stop whatever blessing God has for you.

Remember their third eye is open so they can see your promotion coming.

They can see your blessing.

once that contact is made your blessing, and your promotion is cancelled.

We must know the people we are in fellowship with.

But when we disobey God, your blessing is canceled.

This is what we tell God without speaking it.

we show him that 1Corinthians 12 his gifts and his redemption gifts is not important to be used in their churches.

God had equipped the body of Christ to have these gifts whether they believe it or not.

The gifts are the best weapon against Satan and his kingdom because if the gifts are being used the witches will be exposed the warlocks will be exposed and the body of Christ will have power on high.

The witches are send to keep the power of God out of the churches is it working you tell me.

Printed in the United States
by Baker & Taylor Publisher Services